MW01077455

POCKETBOOKS
by BroadStreet

2-MINUTE DEVOTIONS FOR MEN

BroadStreet

BroadStreet Publishing Group, LLC.
Savage, Minnesota, USA
Broadstreetpublishing.com

2-Minute Devotions for Men
© 2025 by BroadStreet Publishing®

9781424568468
9781424568475 eBook

All rights reserved. No part of this publication may be reproduced, distributed, or transmitted in any form or by any means, including photocopying, recording, or other electronic or mechanical methods, without the prior written permission of the publisher, except in the case of brief quotations embodied in critical reviews and certain other noncommercial uses permitted by copyright law. No portion of this book may be used or reproduced in any way for the purpose of training artificial intelligence technologies. As per Article 4(3) of the Digital Single Market Directive 2019/790, BroadStreet Publishing reserves this work from the text and data mining exception.

Scripture quotations marked NIV are taken from the Holy Bible, New International Version®, NIV®. Copyright © 1973, 1978, 1984, 2011 by Biblica, Inc.™ Used by permission of Zondervan. All rights reserved worldwide. www.zondervan.com. The "NIV" and "New International Version" are trademarks registered in the United States Patent and Trademark Office by Biblica, Inc.™ Scripture quotations marked NLT are taken from the Holy Bible, New Living Translation, copyright ©1996, 2004, 2015 by Tyndale House Foundation. Used by permission of Tyndale House Publishers, Carol Stream, Illinois 60188. All rights reserved. Scripture quotations marked ESV are taken from the ESV® Bible (The Holy Bible, English Standard Version®), Copyright © 2001 by Crossway, a publishing ministry of Good News Publishers. Used by permission. All rights reserved. Scripture quotations marked CSB are taken from the Christian Standard Bible®, Copyright © 2017 by Holman Bible Publishers. Used by permission. Christian Standard Bible® and CSB® are federally registered trademarks of Holman Bible Publishers. Scripture quotations marked NASB are taken from the New American Standard Bible, Copyright 2020 by The Lockman Foundation. Used by permission. All rights reserved. Scripture quotations marked NKJV are taken from the New King James Version®. Copyright © 1982 by Thomas Nelson. Used by permission. All rights reserved. Scripture quotations marked NCV are taken from the New Century Version®. Copyright © 2005 by Thomas Nelson. Used by permission. All rights reserved. Scripture quotations marked TPT are taken from The Passion Translation® of the Holy Bible. Copyright © 2020 by Passion & Fire Ministries, Inc. Used by permission of BroadStreet Publishing®. All rights reserved.

Typesetting and design by Garborg Design Works | garborgdesign.com
Compiled and edited by Michelle Winger | literallyprecise.com

Printed in China.

25 26 27 28 29 30 31   7 6 5 4 3 2 1

The call to discipleship
is a call to death of self.

INTRODUCTION

Life has become increasingly busy. We jump
from one responsibility to the next with little time in
between. We settle for things that satisfy our immediate
needs, but we long for more.

2-Minute Devotions for Men presents 100 quick
meditations for you to reflect on. A moment spent in
God's presence empowers you to be a man of character,
strength, and integrity. Be inspired and refreshed as
you take a break to ponder each Scripture, devotion,
and prayer.

Enjoy this lifegiving interruption that provides
satisfaction beyond your temporary needs and desires,
peace that lightens the load of your responsibilities,
and love that helps you share God's goodness with the
people around you.

PRIORITIES

All glory to God our Father forever and ever!
PHILIPPIANS 4:20 NLT

The temptation we may struggle to overcome is the need for approval, affirmation, or adoration from those around us. We want love and respect from our family members, recognition from coworkers, and good standing within our community. We strive for these conditional social rewards. Something within us longs for acceptance, and so we shift our attention to the accolades this world offers.

If we're not proactive, our priorities can become misguided. We can be tricked into thinking that others should lift us up. It has been said that the chief end of man is to bring glory to God. The honest question that every man needs to face is this: Who do I want to see glorified in my life today?

God, whenever I am swayed to seek my own stance on a pedestal, remind me of who you are and what my priorities should be.

BLESSING

May the grace of the Lord Jesus Christ be with your spirit.
PHILIPPIANS 4:23 NLT

Does anyone in your family or within your network of friends need to receive a blessing like this from you? You're in a privileged and unique situation to speak life into those who need your love. You have the incredible opportunity, through your words, to encourage those closest to you.

God wants you to extend his blessing. So, today, receive the grace he has for you through Jesus and then be intentional about sharing that grace with those you love. Jesus loves you, has given his life for you. He offers you unrelenting relationship. Now do the same for others in his grace-filled power.

God, may you give me more than enough grace, so I overflow on those around me.

CHANGING LIVES

This same Good News that came to you is going out all over the world. It is bearing fruit everywhere by changing lives, just as it changed your lives from the day you first heard and understood the truth about God's wonderful grace.
COLOSSIANS 1:6 NLT

The good news of Jesus is that our sins are forgiven and our relationship with God is restored through his saving work on the cross. This seed, when planted, grows and bears fruit for generations.

You have a remarkable twofold calling. First, you are called to embrace the good news wherever you are, making the grace and truth of Jesus the central component of your life. Second, you are called to share this good news with anyone who comes across your path. Sow the seeds of the gospel of Jesus within their lives. Help them to cultivate their faith. Provide the water, the light, the nutrients, and the environment for their faith to flourish. And watch with joy as the good news of Jesus spreads through them.

God, let me never cover up my faith. Continue to change my life by your Spirit.

WORK SO HARD

We tell others about Christ, warning everyone and teaching everyone with all the wisdom God has given us. We want to present them to God, perfect in their relationship to Christ. That's why I work and struggle so hard, depending on Christ's mighty power that works within me.

COLOSSIANS 1:28-29 NLT

If you were called to a meeting with God, and if it were your special responsibility to introduce the people in your life to him, what would you say? If you had your lifetime to prepare for this meeting, how would you spend your life?

Paul tirelessly invested the qualities of his own life into others. His desire was to present people to God, perfect through Christ. He sought God's wisdom in the practice of his own faith so he would know how to teach and represent God to those he cared about. He worked so hard, not for his own gain but so others would discover and embrace the forgiveness and abundance that comes from knowing Jesus.

God, may the work of my heart and hands today be determined, strong, and courageous.

If Jesus is to be your Lord, let him be your Lord in every way.

CONTINUE TO LIVE

Just as you accepted Christ Jesus as your Lord, you must continue to follow him.
COLOSSIANS 2:6 NLT

Just because at some point in your life you committed yourself to Jesus, it doesn't mean that your faith is to remain static. To be a disciple of Jesus means to be a learner of him.

Continue to follow Jesus. Follow him with more attentive steps than yesterday. Learn his thoughts, his actions, and his will. Seek out his decisions for you, search out his advice, and call out for his wisdom. Run to his healing, walk where he miraculously stands, and get down into the messes in which he so willingly places himself. Embrace him as tightly today as you did at any point in your past. If Jesus is to be your Lord, let him be your Lord in every way.

God, give me the resolve to continue to trust myself to your guidance, your steps, and your presence in my life. I want to follow you again today, as I did yesterday and as I will tomorrow.

DON'T GET CAUGHT

Don't let anyone capture you with empty philosophies and high-sounding nonsense that come from human thinking and from the spiritual powers of this world, rather than from Christ.

COLOSSIANS 2:8 NLT

In Genesis 3, Satan captured Adam and Eve in the Garden of Eden. They bought his shrewd, high-sounding nonsense. In Matthew 4, Satan tried his alluring arguments again, this time to trip up Jesus in the desert. Each statement and question lobbed by Satan was a like a high-arching grenade. If Jesus had taken the bait, the consequences would have been explosive. But he stayed the course. He freely dispatched Satan's empty philosophies by being even shrewder than the snake.

How did he resist while Adam and Eve had fallen? What was Jesus' weapon? It was the uncompromising ballistic missile of truth. Staying alert and on course isn't just for your sake. The arguments you buy and the conclusions you accept impact the generations that follow you.

God, as for me and my family, we will serve you.

NEW NATURE

Put on your new nature, and be renewed as you learn to know your Creator and become like him.
COLOSSIANS 3:10 NLT

In Genesis 1, God merely spoke, and the stars were born. He said, "Let there be …" and there was. In the beginning, Christ was the Word who declared to the darkness that there should be light.

Jesus has spoken into your life today. He declares you free from sin. He proclaims the year of the Lord's favor, release for those who are captured, and sight for those who have lost their vision. He speaks a new vocation for your days. He calls you to him, and he calls you to change the world. His words beckon you to draw near and empower you to move mountains. He asks you to speak with his voice, his authority, his commands, and his creativity. Be refreshed today. Put on the new nature given to you by Jesus, the Creator of the world.

God, refresh me today. Draw me close to you and help me to share this newness of life with those around me.

CONTENT

*I know what it is to be in need, and I know what it is to
have plenty. I have learned the secret of being content
in any and every situation, whether well fed or hungry,
whether living in plenty or in want.*

PHILIPPIANS 4:12 NIV

We often think of contentment as the satisfaction
of all our needs. If that were true, it would only be
possible to be content when everything is perfect. God
gives us the power and the peace to be okay even when
everything around us is not.

Our decision-making and leadership is better
when we learn to be content no matter the outcome.
God frequently reminds us that true peace and
contentment comes from our relationship with him
and not the circumstances of our life.

*God, please give me your perspective on my life. Help me to
be content even when there are things I wish I could change.
Help me to trust that, no matter what, you are enough.*

The intention of your heart is as important as the conduct of your behavior.

WITNESSES

We have all of these great witnesses who encircle us like clouds. So we must let go of every wound that has pierced us and the sin we so easily fall into. Then we will be able to run life's marathon race with passion and determination, for the path has been already marked out before us.

HEBREWS 12:1 TPT

We often perform better when someone is watching. We fight harder, strive further, and endure longer when we know others are paying attention. When we forget we're being watched, it becomes easier to succumb to our struggle. We might rest our defenses and end up tangled in things we wouldn't want others to see.

The everyday people in our lives surround us like a cloud. They are paying attention even when we might think they're not. God cheers for us to wrestle free from the things that would hinder our relationship with them and with him. Our hearts will fight for others more fiercely than we fight for ourselves.

Lord, I desire to be a good example for the people in my life. They are worth any struggle, so please use them to inspire me to keep fighting.

GOD-BREATHED

All Scripture is God-breathed and is useful for teaching, rebuking, correcting and training in righteousness, so that the servant of God may be thoroughly equipped for every good work.

2 TIMOTHY 3:16-17 NIV

There's a mysterious weight to the words of Scripture. It's easy to live with a more-or-less understanding of God's ideal life gleaned from the general idea of a verse. When we forgo the specific words of the Bible, we pull its punches a little bit.

Even though those around us might respond with glazed eyes, it is worth quoting relevant verses at relevant times. When we do, the life God has breathed into those words will help it come alive in the heart of the listener. The entire Bible is available to give just the right wisdom in just the right way.

God, I want to know your Word so I can apply it when opportunities arise. Help me to recall the verses I have read whenever they can be of use in my life or the lives of those around me. Please sharpen my spiritual mind.

OBEDIENCE

*"Go and gather together all the Jews of Susa and fast
for me. Do not eat or drink for three days, night or day.
My maids and I will do the same. And then, though it is
against the law, I will go in to see the king. If I must die,
I must die."*

ESTHER 4:16 NLT

God rarely asks us to produce a specific result.
What he most frequently asks of us is simple
obedience. We don't always know what the result might
be or even what God's will is in a certain moment.
What we can be sure of is that he desires our devotion
and commitment no matter the consequences.

Esther was unsure what would come of her
actions, but she was certain it was what she needed to
do. The result would possibly be death, but her only
concern was obedience. We can miss opportunities to
serve God when we focus on the outcome. God's desire
is to grow us through an experience and to have us trust
him with whatever happens. Life with God is not about
results; it is about obedience.

*God, thank you for inviting me to be a part of what you are
doing in the world.*

DOING GOOD

As for you, brothers, do not grow weary in doing good.
2 THESSALONIANS 3:13 ESV

It is worth it to keep doing what is right and good. It may be thankless and difficult, but it is always worth it. You might feel like it doesn't matter or that nobody notices how hard you work to live how God says to live. Perhaps you feel cheated because, despite your efforts, things just aren't working.

Keep going. Don't grow weary now. It's possible you won't see the results of your devotion, but nothing you give to God is fruitless. Lower your shoulder and keep pressing on. Every decision you make to do what is good gives God one more tool in his toolbox, and he is working to build something amazing in your life.

God, strengthen me to keep living how you ask me to live. Give me the endurance to make the decisions that please you. Restore my energy and help me to keep moving forward.

Your weapon is the
uncompromising
ballistic missile
of truth.

ADDING WORDS

"Every word of God is flawless; he is a shield to those who take refuge in him. Do not add to his words, or he will rebuke you and prove you a liar."
PROVERBS 30:5-6 NIV

When we believe the Bible is on our side, we must take great care in how we convey its truth. It is good to understand what the Bible says about any situation, and following what God says helps us keep our integrity.

However, we must be careful not to exaggerate what Scripture says just because we think we're right. Let Scripture speak for itself. It's not our job to make the listener agree. We can simply share what the Bible says and trust that God will water and grow his truth for his purposes. God delights in our righteousness, but he also yearns for the righteousness of others.

Lord, help me to speak only your truth when helping others to see your light. Please protect me from injecting my own opinions into the work you're trying to do. I want to be an amplifier for your truth.

POINTING

"You search the Scriptures because you think they give you eternal life. But the Scriptures point to me! Yet you refuse to come to me to receive this life."
JOHN 5:39-40 NLT

Approaching Jesus can be intimidating. We're often afraid of what he might say, or ask, or already know. This fear will drive us to keep doing the "safer" spiritual discipline of just reading the Bible. Secretly, we hope that rushed prayers and memorized verses won't disrupt our lives too much.

But Jesus wants to disrupt our lives. He wants to shake up our routine and replace the parts that are lacking with the vibrant life we crave in the depths of our soul. Scripture is good precisely because it begs us to intimately connect with our Savior. Don't shy away from the spiritual tug of Scripture. If you let it lead you to Jesus, you will find what are you are looking for in every verse.

God, you want to bring satisfying life to every part of who I am. Remind me that your core desire is for me to experience the life you created me to live.

INFINITELY MORE

All glory to God, who is able, through his mighty power at work within us, to accomplish infinitely more than we might ask or think.

EPHESIANS 3:20 NLT

God delights in surprising us. Like a father building an incredible treehouse for his child or a husband unveiling a dream vacation to his wife, God takes joy in doing things for us that exceed our expectations. He wants us to stare at him in wonder and realize that he is so much more impressive than we give him credit for.

Often our dreams aren't big enough. We'd settle for a response to prayer that helps us just get by. Our heavenly Father wants more than that! We convince ourselves we aren't worth his time, but he says, "I want your life to be abundant, and I'm going to do that through you." The power of God is most beautifully demonstrated in his ability to exceed our expectations by working through us.

God, you are so much better than I can imagine. I know that even my grandest request seems small compared to what you want to accomplish through me.

BIGGER

*I pray that out of his glorious riches he may strengthen you
with power through his Spirit in your inner being, so that
Christ may dwell in your hearts through faith. And I pray
that you, being rooted and established in love, may have
power, together with all the Lord's holy people, to grasp
how wide and long and high and deep is the love of Christ.*
EPHESIANS 3:16-18 NIV

Our understanding of God begins with that first
aha moment where his power becomes reality. That
first taste creates a hunger for more, and we strive to
learn all we can about God. As our understanding of
God grows, so does his stature and power in our mind.

But eventually we realize that God exceeds
our ability to understand. For believers, this is an
invitation to experience God in a way we can't explain.
God's power, working within us, pushes out the
boundaries we've created. God is actively working to
help you experience even deeper satisfaction in your
relationship with him.

*God, thank you that every day is a chance to be amazed by
your character.*

God gives you the
power and the peace
to be okay even when
everything around you
is not.

MENTORED BY MERCY

Fathers, do not make your children angry, but raise them with the training and teaching of the Lord.

EPHESIANS 6:4 NCV

For most people, the first understanding of God is directly connected to how they experienced their earthly father. Fathers are models of God whether they intend to be or not. A child with a strict father will usually first assume God is judgmental. A child with an absent father will often first perceive God as uncaring. Fathers shape the lens through which children first see their Savior.

Through Jesus, God set his example of mercy through mentorship. It's easy to express reactionary anger when we are upset, but the Holy Spirit works to direct that angry energy into opportunities for growth and learning. When we do that, we paint a more accurate picture of God for the people in our lives.

God, I want others to know you. Please help me to conduct myself in a way that makes you look good. I pray that I will choose opportunities for growth over angry outbursts.

NOTHING WITHOUT YOU

"I am the vine; you are the branches. The one who remains in me and I in him produces much fruit, because you can do nothing without me."

JOHN 15:5 CSB

Many times we treat God like a turbo boost for life. For the most part we do our own thing, work hard to achieve our goals, and muscle through each day. But sometimes, when things are really hard, we finally relent and pray that God would help us over some particularly difficult hurdle in life.

If the above verse were written with regard to how many of us live, it would say "apart from me you can do most things." Of course, Jesus knew what he was saying. His point was clear: we shouldn't save our reliance on him like some sort of power-up. We are designed for constant connection to Christ. We function best, and really only function at all, when we choose to connect with God at all times, not just in tough times.

God, thank you for being my source of strength every day. I pray that I will reflexively turn to you in every situation instead of leaning on you only when I've exhausted all other options.

WEARY

Even youths shall faint and be weary, and young men shall fall exhausted; but they who wait for the Lord shall renew their strength; they shall mount up with wings like eagles; they shall run and not be weary; they shall walk and not faint.

ISAIAH 40:30-31 ESV

Whenever you feel worn out, it should serve as a reminder to connect with God. When we try to do things with our own power, we often find ourselves drained before the task is accomplished. But when we trust that God is at work and we are simply assisting him, we find a deep supply of energy to keep doing his will.

The next time you're exhausted, pause and talk to God. He may encourage you to keep going, he may insist you stop worrying and rest, or he may convict you to shed the added weight. No matter how he responds, he promises to help you keep going in a way you might have thought impossible before.

Lord, thank you for giving me strength and energy when I feel I'm running out. Help me to continue experiencing your goodness even when I'm weary.

COMFORT

Even when I go through the darkest valley,
I fear no danger,
for you are with me;
your rod and your staff—they comfort me.
PSALM 23:4 CSB

President Theodore Roosevelt famously said, "Speak softly and carry a big stick." Sometimes we focus too much on the gentle and comforting shepherd image of God, forgetting that one of the primary jobs of a shepherd is defender, which he is prepared to do.

It is in the darkest and most terrifying places that we are keenly aware of our source of safety. As our fight-or-flight reaction kicks in, we pay attention to anything that offers protection. Perhaps this is the reason God sometimes leads us through dark periods of life, so we are reminded of the safety found in him. Your heavenly Father has every intention of protecting you with his might, and that fact should bring you deep peace when you're afraid.

God, thank you for protecting me. Thank you for leading me through things that are intimidating and for promising to help me fight when the time comes.

The life God has breathed into his Word will come alive in the heart of the listener.

WORSHIP THE SPLENDOR

Honor the LORD for the glory of his name.
Worship the LORD in the splendor of his holiness.
The voice of the LORD echoes above the sea.
The God of glory thunders.
PSALM 29:2-3 NLT

Worshiping God is the only natural response to his power. When we find ourselves in seasons where worship is difficult, we can think it's because we don't feel close to him. Intimacy is often the result of worship, and worship is the result of focusing on God's power and goodness.

God's might is the source of the good things we experience in him. In times of difficulty, we rely on his strength to protect us. In times of joy, we celebrate his power working within us. In all situations, we benefit from placing our focus on the splendor of God. In doing so we pave the way for a deeper sense of intimacy with and connection to our Creator.

God, you are powerful and mighty. Help me to focus on your characteristics so that I can see my own life with a better perspective.

IMITATE

I urge you to imitate me.
1 CORINTHIANS 4:16 CSB

You're a Christian not just because someone told you about Jesus, but because they also demonstrated what it means to live a Christ-centered life. The person who showed you is also following the example set for them by another, who is in turn copying yet another. For every Christian, there is an unbroken line of imitators that can be traced back to Jesus himself.

Your job is to live in such a way that the chain continues. Is an invitation to live like you also an invitation to live like Jesus? Your imitation becomes an invitation to those around you into a satisfying life.

Lord, help me to live how you taught me to live. I want my life to be an example of what it means to have a life devoted to you.

FULLNESS

May you experience the love of Christ, though it is too
great to understand fully. Then you will be made complete
with all the fullness of life and power that comes from God.
EPHESIANS 3:19 NLT

Christ's love brings fullness of life. It was his love for humanity that pushed him to sacrifice so much on our behalf. It is through that same love that we are invited into a rich and satisfying life. It is Christ's love that is the missing puzzle piece for all those who have yet to follow him.

The promise of Christ's love is that we have been made complete. Our own lives are transformed, and we are able to live with more power and purpose than we ever could alone. Through that power we can help others experience the same amazing love and invite them into the full life God intends for us.

God, please continue pouring into me. Help me to
experience your love in a way that fills my life.

YOUNG EXAMPLES

Let no one despise you for your youth, but set the believers an example in speech, in conduct, in love, in faith, in purity.
1 TIMOTHY 4:12 ESV

It's our job to teach younger believers, and daily we should be looking for ways to explain or model something we wish for them to learn. Perhaps we feel like a faucet of knowledge, pouring out what we know into the young vessels. There is deep satisfaction in seeing what we've taught take hold in the lives of others.

We can easily view it as a one-way street, but while God is using us to teach others, he is also revealing himself to us through them. Some traits of the Lord are best demonstrated through youthful innocence and purity. If we pay close attention, we'll see the nature of God in younger Christians. When you do, celebrate it and encourage them.

God, please give me eyes to see what younger believers can teach me about you. Please remind me to thank them each time they remind me of who you are.

Life with God is not about results; it is about obedience.

CALLED UP

"You should select from all the people able men, God-fearing, trustworthy, and hating dishonest profit. Place them over the people as commanders of thousands, hundreds, fifties, and tens."

EXODUS 18:21 CSB

When God is at work, he recruits men with hearts pointed toward him. He is less concerned about skill and experience and more concerned with motivation and love. Men who are intentionally living for Jesus are the most likely to be called into faithful action.

It is in day-to-day life that people demonstrate their readiness for leadership. A man who waits for his marching orders to begin conditioning will find himself woefully underprepared. Instead, the most useful followers of Jesus are those who put his teachings into practice each day. It is never fruitless to follow Jesus with daily devotion.

God, I want to be the kind of man you can call on when you are at work around me. Please use my everyday experiences to strengthen and grow me into someone who can serve you well.

SAFETY IN NUMBERS

Where there is no guidance, a people falls,
but in an abundance of counselors there is safety.
PROVERBS 11:14 ESV

There is truth to the old saying, "It takes a village to raise a child." Parents can easily fall into the trap of believing that they alone must provide protection and instruction for their children. But living this way robs kids of experiencing the richness of many voices.

We are called to be both discerning and generous with the guidance of children. We should recognize the children that God has placed in our lives and be a part of their village! Then we set an example for Christian community and help their parents to provide a buffet of positive influence for their children. We are called to be a blessing to both our friends and their children.

God, thank you for the opportunity to be a positive voice who speaks into the life of children. I pray you will bless the families that I can influence by my words and actions.

WARNING AND PATIENCE

We urge you, brothers and sisters, warn those who are idle and disruptive, encourage the disheartened, help the weak, be patient with everyone.

1 THESSALONIANS 5:14 NIV

Correction and patience must go hand in hand. Correction without patience is anger. Patience without correction is avoidance. Being a godly leader requires both in equal balance.

The Bible urges us to follow God's example when encouraging right living in others. We are to point out God's expectations and highlight clearly when they're not met. This provides a chance to do the right thing. But the entire process falls apart if not done with encouragement, strength, and patience. These are the three main ingredients of godly direction.

God, when I need to encourage others to live how you say to live, please help me correct them the way you say to correct. Give me the strength and patience to truly encourage change in their lives and continue to change me in the process as well.

TELL THEM

Parents will tell their children what you have done.
They will retell your mighty acts.
PSALM 145:4 NCV

We know an experience has profoundly changed us when we begin telling others about it. There is great power in stories, and the most powerful stories are those of God changing us. Throughout your life, God has worked to bring transformation, blessing, and wisdom.

No doubt each of us has a favorite story. We connect to stories in an incredible way, and the fastest route to a person's heart is through a story. You're an expert in your story, and sharing the ways God has worked in your life is not only your responsibility but also one of the most effective ways of discipleship. Tell people what God has done in your life.

God, please help me to be authentic in talking with others about how you are at work. I want them to know you by hearing about the work you are doing in me.

The power of
God is beautifully
demonstrated in his
ability to exceed our
expectations.

EVERYTHING YOU DO

*Encourage the young men to live wisely. And you yourself
must be an example to them by doing good works of
every kind. Let everything you do reflect the integrity and
seriousness of your teaching.*
TITUS 2:6-7 NLT

The only way to demonstrate that we really mean
what we say is to live it. Our actions are our primary
way of teaching; our own lives are the ultimate visual
aid for any life lesson we try to convey. If we want
people to listen to our advice, we must live it clearly for
them to see.

But if we want them to listen to our advice, we
must also speak it. The best way to instruct is the one-
two punch of teaching and modeling. We must live
correctly and then explain why we have chosen to live
that way. People around you will learn from your life no
matter what it teaches.

*God, please help me to be consistent in what I teach to the
people in my life. Give me the strength and wisdom so my
life can serve as a wonderful lesson of what it means to be a
man of God.*

Rest

*It is useless for you to work so hard from early morning
until late at night, anxiously working for food to eat;
for God gives rest to his loved ones.*

Psalm 127:2 nlt

Failure to rest is usually the result of failure to trust
God. There are many valid things we could do with any
hour of the day, and danger comes when we forget that
rest is one of them. We were created to rest; in fact, the
first full day that Creator and man spent together was a
day of rest.

We know God disapproves of laziness, but we
often forget that it is also sinful to never rest. No
amount of work will ever supply the deep sleep and
rest that God offers. He beckons us to rest so we can
remember our dependence on him. When we do, we
are more likely to depend on him on the busy days as
well. Take time today to rest.

*Lord, give me the courage to make time for rest by delaying
or declining the things I need to do. Please provide peace
that everything will be okay if I take time and obey your
command to rest.*

KNOW YOUR FLOCK

Be sure you know the condition of your flocks,
give careful attention to your herds.
PROVERBS 27:23 NIV

It's not enough to simply watch for trouble in the
lives of our friends and family. We are called to keep
our finger on the pulse of their heart and soul. We
can easily lose that pulse in the normal rhythm of our
everyday relationships. We must give special care to
our flock: the people in our care.

The beauty is that when trouble comes, we're more
prepared for it. In fact, we're likely to catch it earlier
if we already know the condition of another person's
spiritual life. We're called to diligently keep watch over
the ups and downs in the lives of the people we care
most about.

God, please give me the ability to sense how my friends and
family are doing spiritually. Help me remain consistent in
my attention to their lives. Please highlight the things you
want me to see.

ACT JUSTLY

He has shown you, O man, what is good;
and what does the LORD require of you.
but to do justly, to love mercy,
and to walk humbly with your God?

MICAH 6:8 NKJV

God has shown us what is good. Not merely through his law, although his law is good. Not only by dealing with those who reject those laws. Not only by keeping his Word. God shows us what is good through his Son, Jesus. Jesus was the physical representation of justice. He brought healing. He brought freedom. He brought hope. He righted wrongs. And, finally, he paid the penalty for our sin in an ultimate act of justice.

We act justly when we behave as Jesus did. To act justly is to remember that we love others because Jesus first loved us. God's justice is not only final, but also complete. And it is utterly hope filled.

Lord, you've shown me what is good, in your Word and in your actions. Teach me to act justly in a world that so desperately needs it.

Fathers shape the lens through which children first see their Savior.

SELF-SACRIFICE

"The Kingdom of Heaven is like a treasure that a man discovered hidden in a field. In his excitement, he hid it again and sold everything he owned to get enough money to buy the field."

MATTHEW 13:44 NLT

We sacrifice the most for the things we most desire. We will commit to a thirty-year loan to own a home and to a six-year loan for an automobile. We work forty, fifty, even sixty hours a week (or more) to get a promotion at work. And with each of these things comes a cost.

There is, however, something greater than any of the above. God's kingdom. Jesus tells us that God's kingdom is so valuable that it would be like finding a treasure hidden in a field, then selling everything we own to buy that field to get the treasure. What might it look like for us to pursue God's kingdom with such intensity?

God, I have experienced the glory of your kingdom, and I want it to be my life's greatest pursuit. Please help me honestly evaluate my sacrifice for you.

MOST IMPORTANT LESSON

"This is how God loved the world: He gave his one and only son, so that everyone who believes in him will not perish but have eternal life."

JOHN 3:16 NLT

This text is likely the most recognizable text in the Bible, if not in the English language. You will see it in the end zone at a football game, behind the catcher at a baseball game, behind the backboard at a basketball game, and along the racetrack at a car race. It is held high in a town parade by churches and individuals alike. Why?

Because in it we find the most important lesson that there is: God loved us so much that he sent his Son, Jesus, to perish in our place. This is the gospel message in one simple sentence. Of all the things that we learn in life, it is this message that is the most important.

Father, you loved me so much that sent your Son to pay for my sins. Teach me to be grateful for it and to pass it on.

IDENTITY

You are no longer a slave but a son, and if a son, then God has made you an heir.
GALATIANS 4:7 CSB

This is no small change of identity. From slave to son is a huge change. We are given the right status to walk hand in hand with our heavenly Father. We don't follow him around out of obligation but instead walk with him as he calls us.

The relationship we are given with God through Christ is an amazing opportunity to sit with God and converse, to hug, and to see the smile that only a father can give a child. A smile that says, "That man there is my son. I love him and am proud of him."

Thank you, God, for calling me your son. Thank you that you smile upon me and call me your own. When I am discouraged, remind me that I am your child, and you have all that I need.

DON'T SHRINK

"I never shrank back from telling you what you needed to hear, either publicly or in your homes."
ACTS 20:20 NLT

As Paul was preparing to leave the elders from Ephesus, he essentially gave them his resignation notice. He told them that he loved them and that from day one it was his desire that they know Jesus. He spoke of his hard work among them, and how this often required confronting them with truth. Confronting others is one of the most difficult things that we do. When the person we will confront is a family member, it is even more difficult. But confrontation is part of being a man. It is necessary.

When it came to telling people what they needed to hear, Paul did not shrink back. We must not be afraid to be honest with people and speak truth. What they need to hear beyond any other message is the truth of the gospel and the good news of Jesus Christ.

I am thankful for the people in my life who did not shrink back from telling me a truth that I needed to hear. Please give me that same courage.

You function best
when you choose to
connect with God
at all times.

HONORING PARENTS

Children, obey your parents because you belong to the Lord, for this is the right thing to do. "Honor your father and mother." This is the first commandment with a promise: If you honor your father and mother, "things will go well for you, and you will have a long life on the earth."
EPHESIANS 6:1-3 NLT

As children, we were under the authority of our parents and had to obey them. But in that obedience, we may or may not have honored them; this was determined by our attitude. As adults, while we are no longer bound to obey our parents, we are supposed to honor them.

We honor our parents when we ask for advice, when we speak kindly of them, when we spend time with them, and when we defer to them. This demonstrates respect, value, and humility, and it shows others how to honor their parents.

Lord, my parents have taught me so much about life. Help me to honor their efforts by respecting and valuing them in ways that others see, so they will be blessed.

HOPE

The same thing is true of the words I speak.
They will not return to me empty.
They make the things happen that I want to happen,
and they succeed in doing what I send them to do.
ISAIAH 55:11 NCV

As godly men, we look for ways to teach and train others in the faith. We offer to take them to church, join our small group, or do something as simple as sharing a meal so they can talk about their struggles and doubts. We pray for and with them. Even so, they sometimes make decisions that lead them away from Jesus. We are crushed, heartbroken, and frustrated. Does this sound familiar?

This Scripture teaches us that the faithfulness of God's Word is ever fruitful. His words are not pie-in-the-sky naiveté but truth. Promises. Believable. Inspiring. Trustworthy. Full and complete. And they do everything that God sends them to do.

Father, I so much want people to know who you are. I praise and thank you for your words of hope.

COURAGE

Be watchful, stand firm in the faith, act like men, be strong.
Let all that you do be done in love.
1 CORINTHIANS 16:13-14 ESV

There is a crisis of fatherhood today. The US Census Bureau says 24 million children (one in three) live in homes without their own dad. But children with dads involved in their life are more successful, more confident, more sociable, and less likely to have a list of adolescent problems. Clearly, dads play a large role in the success of children. These truths not only apply to biological fathers, but men who are willing to be spiritual fathers as well.

This verse includes four descriptions of a godly man. He is alert, stands firm in the faith, is strong in his courage, and loving. It's a challenging list! It takes courage to be a godly man, and even more so to be a godly "father." What younger men has God placed in your life who are in desperate need of a spiritual father?

God, being a spiritual father is an amazing privilege. With your help, I'm up for the challenge because people need me. Help me to be a man that makes a difference.

ENCOURAGE

Fathers, do not provoke your children, lest they become discouraged.

COLOSSIANS 3:21 NKJV

The truth of this verse extends far beyond the relationship that a father has with his son. As men of God, we should not provoke anyone. Earlier in this chapter, Paul told the Colossians to "put off" the things that lead to spiritual death: anger, wrath, malice, blasphemy, and lying. Each of these behaviors are provoking in nature. When we respond in these ways to the people in our lives, we are bound to discourage them.

Put on mercy, kindness, humility, meekness, patience, forgiveness, and love. Be ruled by the peace of God. Let his words live within you and do everything in his name. When we do not provoke others, we encourage them to come to us and live out our example. Be an encourager!

Father, help me evaluate the way I speak with the people around me. I want to be encouraging. Give me opportunities to be humble, forgiving, peaceful, and kind.

God recruits men
with hearts pointed
toward him.

EAT MEAT

You are like babies who need milk and cannot eat solid food. For someone who lives on milk is still an infant and doesn't know how to do what is right. Solid food is for those who are mature, who through training who have the skill to recognize the difference between right and wrong.

HEBREWS 5:12-14 NLT

There's nothing like a properly cooked piece of meat. After we have eaten it, we feel satisfied. As we get older, our eating habits change, and we adjust. What made us feel full at one barely makes a dent in our hunger when we are seven. And when we are seventeen? Forget it. Keeping up with that appetite is nearly impossible!

The same is true with spiritual nourishment. When we were young, we received spiritual milk; we were introduced to main Bible characters and stories. But as we got older, we started digging into meatier concepts like salvation, sanctification, and justification. What have you been feeding yourself lately? Are you still drinking from a bottle, or do you have your steak knife ready?

God, help me see how hungry I am. I need more of you.

THE CLOSEST FISH

Then he said to them, "Follow me, and I will make you fishers of men."
MATTHEW 4:19 NKJV

A lot of work goes into catching fish. We need to have all the right equipment. If you don't want to fish from a dock or the shore, you'll need a boat. After accumulating all the gear, you'll be faced with the toughest decisions of all: where to fish and when. Often, we make these decisions by asking others. Who wants to go fishing and catch nothing?

When Jesus spoke to his earliest disciples, he invited them to go fishing with him. Rather than go away to a far-off place, Jesus and the disciples fished for men throughout the region of Galilee. At the end of his ministry, Jesus told his followers to go out and make disciples, beginning nearby in Jerusalem and then spreading to the ends of the earth. We have fish near us. They are the people we interact with every day.

God, I can be a fisher of men as well. Help me to see that you have given me all I need to catch them for you.

LOVED BY HIM

"The Lord disciplines those he loves, and he punishes each one he accepts as his child."

HEBREWS 12:6 NLT

"This hurts me more than it will hurt you." As a child you may have heard this phrase. Parents know the truth of this statement because, while discipline is part of being a parent, it is not a joyous one. Being corrected should not be vengeful punishment, but loving discipline. Loving discipline has one goal in mind: restoration. It seeks to bring people together, to right wrongs, to show that justice is possible, and to point to a time of peace.

The greatest example of this is God's love for us. He disciplines us through the consequences of our actions and choices, through the Scriptures, and by conviction from the Holy Spirit. He allows consequences because his desire is for us to be restored to him. This discipline reveals that we are not only loved by him, but that we belong to him.

Father, I am thankful for your discipline. It is designed to restore me to you and to make me more like your Son.

DIVINE DISCIPLINE

As you endure this divine discipline, remember that God is treating you as his own children. Who ever heard of a child not disciplined by its father?

HEBREWS 12:7 NLT

Who ever heard of a child not disciplined by his father? The question asked in this verse is rhetorical, regardless of the answer. On one hand, our response is that discipline of children is part of the parental responsibility." On the other, we say we knew kids who ran wild and caused all sorts of problems. You may have kids on your street whose parents never confront their behavior.

When God disciplines us, he is showing to everyone that we are his. The fact that we endure it is evidence that we are in the hands of a loving father. By default, a father must discipline his child. If not disciplined, the child seemingly belongs to no one.

God, you set the example for discipline. You allow me to endure it first because I need it, and second because it shows that you are indeed a loving father.

God's justice
is not only final,
it is also complete.

STAY ALERT

Be sober, be vigilant; because your adversary the devil walks
about like a roaring lion, seeking whom he may devour.
1 PETER 5:8 NKJV

The word *sober* in this verse has nothing to do with
alcohol or drunkenness; here it means to have a clear
mind, to be alert. To be vigilant means to be looking
both outward and inward for something, to be ready.
But ready for what? The adversary. Our enemy, the devil.

Sometimes we believe that this adversary is out
sneaking around, hiding in the bushes, or creeping up
on us. But the imagery used here is that of a roaring
lion. We know he is coming. In fact, he is announcing
himself. We hear him. The soberness and vigilance is
not about looking for him to arrive, but about being
prepared for his arrival. God works with us, so we not
only know the roar, but we also know what to do when
he arrives.

Lord, my adversary is coming. I know he is because I can
hear him. Help me to be sober and clear minded. Help me
to be vigilant and ready.

JUST ONE GENERATION

When all that generation had been gathered to their fathers, another generation arose after them who did not know the LORD nor the work which He had done for Israel.

JUDGES 2:10 NKJV

A lot can happen in one generation. Nations rise and fall. Resources can be increased or lost forever. Throughout Deuteronomy, we see God giving many instructions to Moses, and in many instances these instructions ended with God saying something like, "And when your children ask about why you do this, tell them that I delivered you out of slavery." The reason given was simple: to keep the people from forgetting what God had done. In just one generation, the knowledge of the past was gone. The people still had the rituals, but they didn't know why.

It's our role to talk about the amazing things God does. We give glory and praise him for his deeds and work. We talk about the why because we need constant reminders of who God is. Let's keep talking about what God has done so the next generation remembers.

Father, help me to remember your love and sacrifice, and to share with others the hope of deliverance.

WASHING FEET

He got up from the table, took off his robe, wrapped a towel around his waist, and poured water into a basin. Then he began to wash the disciples' feet, drying them with the towel he had around him.

JOHN 13:4-5 NLT

Jesus was a servant. He demonstrated this with his disciples the night before he died. After they entered the room where he would eat his final meal, he picked that moment to do the lowliest task a servant could do—wash feet. Jesus did this not out of false humility or to receive praise.

Men can wear a lot of hats: friend, co-worker, boss, son, brother, father, uncle, just to name a few. There are so many people in our lives we are called to serve and love. One of the easiest ways to share the gospel with them and to teach them the character of God is to serve them in the way Jesus served. Each day, we have opportunities to wash the feet of those around us through selfless, and sometimes humiliating, acts of service.

God, I am here to serve you. When I serve the people in my life with honesty and humility, I magnify you alone.

DISCERNMENT

"You must distinguish between the unclean and the clean."
LEVITICUS 11:47 NIV

Beginning in Genesis 3, we find humanity struggling to discern the difference between evil and good, and it is in this struggle that we find people making choices that separate them from God and other people. Cain failed to bring God a righteous offering. David didn't look away from Bathsheba. And while his son Solomon asked for (and received) wisdom from God, he was led astray. In the New Testament, we find Peter refusing to eat with Gentile believers.

We are no different. In Romans 12, we're told to be transformed by the renewing of our minds. These new minds teach us the difference between right and wrong, and then the Holy Spirit gives us the ability to choose what is right. As we pray for knowledge and wisdom, may we also ask for the desire to do the right thing.

God, your Word is clear about right and wrong. Through it, show and teach me what obedience looks like, and give me the courage to do what is good.

Keep talking about
what God has done,
so the next generation
remembers.

PHYSICAL TOUCH

The LORD said to Moses, "Take Joshua son of Nun, a man in whom is the spirit, and lay your hand on him. Give him some of your authority so the whole Israelite community will obey him."

NUMBERS 27:18, 20 NIV

Physical contact affirms what is being verbally communicated. We tell those we care about, "I love you" and often follow it with a hug, kiss, or pat on the back. When parents want a child's attention they may place their hand on their shoulder to indicate their seriousness. Touch can provide a feeling of security.

In Numbers, Moses is told by God to bring Joshua before the people and to lay his hand on him, showing approval as power shifts. In 1 Timothy 4, Paul tells Timothy that he received his gifts when the elders laid hands on him. As men, we must recognize the need for both verbal and physical communication. May we remember the power of loving, kind, appropriate, and frequent touch.

Father, you are a God of touch. When Jesus was on the earth, he healed many by touching them. Help me to value the power of touch.

LONG-TERM PLANS

Salmon begot Boaz, and Boaz begot Obed; Obed begot
Jesse, and Jesse begot David.
RUTH 4:21-22 NKJV

What began as the story of a woman in search
of someone to care for her daughter-in-law ended
twenty-eight generations later with Jesus Christ. Boaz
had no way of knowing this when he took Ruth as his
wife. God, however, knew exactly what he was doing
because he is interested in long-term plans.

Long-term plans are why God considered the
character of those whom he chose—and chooses—to
lead his people. Long-term plans are why Gamliel,
who spoke up in defense of the apostles in Acts 5:33,
was also the mentor of Paul. We have no idea what
God will do with us, our children, our grandchildren,
and beyond. We participate in those plans when we
are obedient today because we set each following
generation on a trajectory of future obedience.

God, you are all-powerful, in every place, and all-knowing.
You alone know what the future holds and the role that I
will play. Help me to choose obedience today.

PREPARATION

Remember your Creator in the days of your youth.
ECCLESIASTES 12:1 NIV

Life is a journey, and it's a trip we only take once. Each of us is on our own path. We cannot turn back time but can only move forward. With that irreversible permanence in mind, how important it is to be careful! And that is why the Bible instructs us to remember our Creator and seek first his kingdom.

In all career paths, there is a requirement of training and preparation. Future doctors study for many years to prepare for their career. Imagine a doctor saying, "I intend to practice medicine, but I have no desire to listen to what others have researched." Certainly not! How foolish would we be not to listen to God's wisdom. Take time to read and learn God's principles that are intended to prepare us for daily life.

Father, you have given me wisdom and truth to follow. Thank you for the gift of your words in the Bible. Create in me the desire to obey you in all things.

WELL DONE

*"His master replied, 'Well done, good and faithful servant!
You have been faithful with a few things; I will put you
in charge of many things. Come and share your master's
happiness!'"*

MATTHEW 25:23 NIV

There is only so much one can accomplish in a
given day. There are twenty-four hours in a day, and in
that time, a number of things need to be done: sleep,
eat, work, spend time with family, and praise God.

How can we do each of these things with the
purpose of glorifying God and being faithful to him?
God has put us in charge of just a few things. The way to
join in the happiness of God is to be faithful in the few
things he has given us and take full advantage of every
moment of each day. Then we will hear, "Well done."

*God, time passes by so quickly that at the end of the day,
I sometimes wonder where it went. Each day is a gift, and
every moment an opportunity for faithfulness. Help me to
serve you each day.*

A follower of
Christ is a strategic
representative of God.

STAND STRONG

Keep yourselves in God's love as you wait for the mercy of our Lord Jesus Christ to bring you eternal life. Be merciful to those who doubt; save others by snatching them from the fire; to others show mercy mixed with fear—hating even the clothing stained by corrupt flesh.

JUDE 21-23 NIV

Waiting for things is not only an important part of life, doing so with patience is a trait of a believer in God. We are in the space between the resurrection and return of Christ, and as we wait, we show mercy and hate evil.

People all have different temperaments and personalities. Perhaps you work with someone who is anxious and filled with doubts; be merciful, gracious, and kind—always. Maybe one of your friends is in grave danger; act decisively and quickly, for time is of the essence. God is merciful to us and has placed people in our lives that we might love them well.

Father, I need your mercy. Make me aware of your mercy that I may be merciful.

WHAT YOU WEAR

*Since God chose you to be the holy people he loves, you
must clothe yourselves with tenderhearted mercy, kindness,
humility, gentleness, and patience.*
COLOSSIANS 3:12 NLT

What kind of clothes should a man wear? A suit
and tie for an important meeting? A uniform for work?
Maybe a ratty T-shirt and jeans for oil changes and
mowing? Or how about some casual Saturday clothes
with his favorite team logo for the sporting event?

The mixture of polyester and cotton isn't nearly as
important as what a man wears in his heart and actions.
Whether we like it or not, a follower of Christ is a
strategic representative of God. What a Christian says
and does has significant ramifications. When we put
on mercy in the midst of trouble, or choose patience
over raising our voices in frustration, or consistently
encourage those around us, it will point people to a
loving God.

*God, help me to be clothed in your qualities and
characteristics today. Let me be a proper representative to
those around me.*

DEVOTED TO PRAYER

Devote yourselves to prayer with an alert mind and a thankful heart.

COLOSSIANS 4:2 NLT

Stop everything you're doing, even if just for a few minutes, and pray. Put aside your anxieties, put to rest your weighted burdens, and have a conversation with God. Take a moment to pray for your relationship with God. What has he done in your life that makes you thankful? What needs could you put in his hands? Take a moment to ask God what his plans are for you.

Take a moment to pray for the people in your life. What has God done in them that makes you thankful? What requests and what needs do they have that you could entrust to the Lord's hands? Take a moment to ask God what he sees when he looks upon them.

God, remind me to be constantly talking with you. Don't let me neglect coming to you in prayer. May I become a devoted man of prayer for not only my own sake, but also for the sake of others.

EVERY OPPORTUNITY

Live wisely among those who are not believers, and make the most of every opportunity. Let your conversation be gracious and attractive so that you will have the right response for everyone.

COLOSSIANS 4:5-6 NLT

Who around you needs God? Take a deep breath, close your eyes, and consider those who are close to you who are not following God. Is there someone in your family? Perhaps one of your friends? A coworker? A neighbor?

Having the right response for someone is not really about knowing how to win an argument. It's much more about living in such a way through the circumstances of life that others take notice. You want others to see a wellspring of strength and a daily resource in you. Be ready to share the source of your strength and courage in everyday moments.

God, let me live consistently in your patterns every day, so I may be ready to share at any moment how great you are.

Put aside your anxieties,
put to rest your
weighted burdens, and
have a conversation
with God.

REPRESENTATIVE

We are Christ's ambassadors; God is making his appeal through us. We speak for Christ when we plead, "Come back to God!"

2 CORINTHIANS 5:20 NLT

There was a king who came to a land and did many good things for the people. This king supplied daily bread, extended mercy to those in trouble, and gave himself on behalf of those in his kingdom. Then, the king asks you to become his representative to those people. In effect, he is calling you to be his ambassador. He is entrusting you with his authority and words.

When you would speak, the words you choose represent the king's words. When you would act, the patterns of your life enact the king's grace or justice. It would be as if the king were right there, living through you. This is how you should live for Christ—as his representative.

God, let me speak as you would speak, act as you would act, and represent you to everyone I come in contact with.

STRONGER TOGETHER

Two are better than one, because they have a good return for their labor: If either of them falls down, one can help the other up. But pity anyone who falls and has no one to help them up.
ECCLESIASTES 4:9-10 NIV

Strength is so often defined as a man who needs no help. Our culture celebrates the stoic man who is able to face his battles singlehandedly. We see the lone wolf celebrated as the ultimate in masculine strength. Ironically, such a man is likely the weakest and most vulnerable type of man you'll find.

Only weak people believe that receiving help is a sign of weakness. In the same way that we delight in offering strength to others, there are others who are eager to offer their strength to us. We need only be courageous enough to seek help, and to keep seeking until we find it. When we do, we will find our strength multiplied by those we join with.

Lord, please keep me from believing the lie that I have to do things on my own. Help me to trust others to carry the weights of my life with me, just as I work to help others with their burdens.

WHAT'S INSIDE

The LORD said to Samuel, "Do not look on his appearance
or on the height of his stature, because I have rejected
him. For the LORD sees not as man sees: man looks on the
outward appearance, but the LORD looks on the heart."
1 SAMUEL 16:7 ESV

God often chooses the unexpected man to
accomplish his goals. This is because God's method of
choosing tends to be much different, and much deeper,
than how we tally the score. The only person we're
likely to assess accurately is ourselves, and even then,
we often exchange God's criteria for one less fitting.

God is able to look at our hearts, and he often
uncovers positive traits even we have overlooked. He
draws out of us a deeper strength than we thought we
possessed. He produces from us more than we thought
ourselves capable of. God is actively working to draw
the very best out of the core of who he made you to be.

God, help me to see myself and others the way you see me.
Please grow in my heart the qualities you desire and keep
me from focusing on traits that don't matter.

COMPLETELY NEW

*If anyone is in Christ, he is a new creation; the old has
passed away, and see, the new has come!*
2 CORINTHIANS 5:17 CSB

The promise of the Christian life is not a better life
or an improved life. The promise of following Jesus is a
completely new life! The transforming power of God is
so strong that it actively erases our old desires and ways
of thinking. It is when we forget this that we start to
beat ourselves up. We carry the weight of our mistakes
around, which slows our growth.

You are a new creation, having been made new
simply by choosing to follow Jesus. You don't need to
worry about your past any longer. Just keep living in
the direction of Jesus.

*God, thank you for making me new. I'm grateful that you
did more than just polish me up or make me presentable;
you completely re-created my way of living. Please help me
to remember the powerful work you've done in me.*

In the act of retreating to God, you make great advances against the enemy.

STRONGHOLD

The LORD is good,
a stronghold in a day of distress;
he cares for those who take refuge in him.
NAHUM 1:7 CSB

In order for God to protect us, we must run to him. God is good, and he promises to offer us safety in times of trouble. The deal is, we must go to him. We need to actively seek his help when trouble comes.

He does this so we keep in mind the true source of strength. In the act of retreating to God, we make great advances against our enemy. In turning to the stronghold, we deal an incredible strike against everything meant to harm us. How can it harm us if it is what brings us closer to our Savior?

God, you are the true strength in my life. Thank you for using potentially harmful things as a way to bring me closer to you.

WORKING IN YOU

God is working in you, giving you the desire and the power to do what pleases him.
PHILIPPIANS 2:13 ESV

God does not give us a list of demands and leave us to sort it out. He uses his power to help strengthen us. He is both the motivation and the destination for our spiritual lives.

We can make the mistake of thinking we must please him in order to experience closeness with him when, in fact, the inverse is what happens. When we draw close to him, he begins to produce in us the desire to do what pleases him.

Lord, I confess I sometimes avoid you because I'm afraid I'm not living how you want me to live. I pray you will help me realize that you are the source of the daily strength I need to live for you. Help me to come to you so you can grow healthy desires in me.

PEACE AND STRENGTH

The LORD gives his people strength.
The LORD blesses them with peace.
PSALM 29:11 NLT

Strength and peace are two things we often think of as being created from within. Inner strength and inner peace are common phrases. While it's true that we perhaps experience those things internally, the source of them is both external and eternal. God gives us strength and blesses us with peace.

When we go through challenging times, we can be tempted to dig deep inside ourselves to find the strength to carry on. The truth is we should reach out to the source of that strength. If we feel we have nothing left, it's a sign that we are looking in the wrong place for peace or perseverance. The wonderful news is there is an endless supply, and God wants to bless us with it.

God, thank you for giving me strength to face difficult challenges. And thank you for going even further and offering peace in incredibly hard times.

WISDOM

With God are wisdom and might;
he has counsel and understanding.

JOB 12:13 ESV

It's no accident that God is the supplier of everything we need in life, be it strength, peace, or wisdom. When the Creator set up the universe, he did it in a way that we would be naturally drawn to him at every turn.

God and wisdom are one and the same. As the Creator, God is innately correct, wise, and right. Because of this, when we are closely aligned with our heavenly Father, we are more likely to know which decisions we need to make. The act of decision-making becomes an act of worship as we rely on our relationship with God to lead the way.

God, I am glad your wisdom and understanding are so great. And I am thankful that you choose to use your power to help me live how you created me to live.

God is both the
motivation and
destination of your
spiritual life.

GROWING GOOD

Let us not become weary in doing good, for at the proper time we will reap a harvest if we do not give up.

GALATIANS 6:9 NIV

Every time we make the decision to do good, we start a countdown until the inevitable moment when we ask, "Is it worth it?" If we're honest, there are plenty of days when it feels like doing good isn't everything it's cracked up to be. People don't notice, life is still hard, and sometimes it seems like more trouble than it's worth.

Don't give up. Each time you do good, a seed is planted, and a life centered around Jesus causes those seeds to grow. We usually don't know the result of every good deed, but we can trust that God does and that he is helping them grow to their fullest potential. The more seeds of good you plant in your life, the more likely it is for your life to become vibrant and full.

God, sometimes I grow tired of working to do what is right; it often feels like an unfair fight. Please help me to trust that you are working through me.

SPEAKING LIFE

"Don't be afraid," he said, "for you are very precious to God. Peace! Be encouraged! Be strong!" As he spoke these words to me, I suddenly felt stronger and said to him, "Please speak to me, my lord, for you have strengthened me."

DANIEL 10:19 NLT

God's words bring life. Whether they come through Scripture, through family or friends, or from some unexpected place, they have the power to invigorate us. When we actively search for what God is speaking, we will find a vitality we might otherwise miss.

We can also speak those words to others to bring them life. We may be hesitant to intrude with Scripture says to our family or friends, but we should be courageous enough to speak life to them as well. God has gifted us with the wonderful power of his words, and he encourages us to share them freely.

God, thank you for speaking life to me. Your words have the power to heal, direct, and strengthen. Please help me to share timely wisdom from you.

CHOSEN

You are a chosen race, a royal priesthood, a holy nation,
a people for his possession, so that you may proclaim the
praises of the one who called you out of darkness into his
marvelous light. Once you were not a people, but now you
are God's people; you had not received mercy, but now you
have received mercy.

1 PETER 2:9-10 CSB

God intentionally picked you. He didn't settle
for you, and he didn't begrudgingly accept you; he
chose you on purpose and for a purpose. You have
been called into a role of great significance; you're an
ambassador for Jesus Christ himself.

You're invited to tell anyone who will listen of
the great change God has brought in you. You're
encouraged to explain that such transformation is
available to them as well. You have an endless supply of
spiritual VIP passes to hand out. Let others know how
important they are to God.

Father, thank you for choosing me. Please give me
opportunities to tell others about the life you have for them.

HOPE

Hope deferred makes the heart sick,
but a dream fulfilled is a tree of life.
PROVERBS 13:12 NLT

Don't put off hope. It's far too easy for our worries to shush the dreaming voice that asks, "What if?" We then delay in pursuing our deepest desires under the guise of safety or prudence. God invites us into adventure, and we reply with a maybe. Replacing hope with waiting leads to an unhealthy life.

True peace comes from seizing the invitation to live a God-centered life. It almost always requires risk, but the reward is the rich and satisfying life we were created to live. People will not be shaped by a maybe, but they will be forever transformed by daring to ask, "What if?"

God, I want to chase the dreams you've instilled in me. Please help me to fulfill the purpose you have for me.

God chose you on
purpose for a purpose.

DEPENDENCE ON CHRIST

God chose what is foolish in the world to shame the wise;
God chose what is weak in the world to shame the strong.
1 CORINTHIANS 1:27 ESV

As a man, you'll need to showcase not strength but life-dependent weakness to the Creator of the universe. People don't need a superman who can fix all the unsolvable problems of the world; they need a committed, God-structured man who lives his life on his knees in total submission to the Lord.

They need to see the air you breathe, the bread you eat, the God who leads your life, and the obedience that comes by faith. Be intentional about living dependently and relying on the strength of God.

Heavenly Father, teach me to live my life in total dependence.
May your Spirit align me with your Word and may my
heart's affection be stirred to your truth.

PROCRASTINATION

If a man is lazy, the rafters sag;
if his hands are idle, the house leaks.
ECCLESIASTES 10:18 NIV

It may seem harsh, but laziness is a learned behavior. You might clear your dishes as soon as you're done eating and put them right in the dishwasher. Or you might leave your dirty dishes lying around and only wash them once you are looking for a plate to use. One is a disciplined behavior, and one reeks of procrastination. Both are learned with practice.

It takes time to develop a disciplined approach to household chores. It also takes time to develop patterns of procrastination. The good news is, if you've learned to be a fantastic procrastinator, you can also learn to be a wonderfully disciplined, proactive man.

Lord Jesus, grant me the power to change the ways in which I've let procrastination become my norm.

TEACH WITH TRAJECTORY

Set your minds on things that are above, not on things that are on earth.

COLOSSIANS 3:2 ESV

With the instantaneous lures of the world, we need to see the value of viewing life through the lens of trajectory. We need to understand the truth that the choices made today impact the pathways for tomorrow, and that life is not merely what our eyes can see, but what the Lord has promised.

And yet, we don't just look toward the future but set our minds on eternity. The love, compassion, sacrifice, and service forged in these days for the sake of the gospel will have a ripple effect for eternity.

Father God, I praise you for the salvation you grant to me through the Lord Jesus Christ. It is by his work that my eternal destiny has been forever changed. Help me to live my life with eternity in view.

CHARACTER

I therefore, a prisoner for the Lord, urge you to walk in a
manner worthy of the calling to which you have been called.
EPHESIANS 4:1 ESV

Walking with integrity and character is the hallmark of the Christian faith. Not that we can merit salvation. But the fruit of our salvation produces in us a coherence to the commandments of God. Our call to salvation is not to an isolation away from God's decree, but rather to exemplify his character, quality, and virtue.

The father's decree is to lead his children not toward individualism, but rather to be a unique image bearer that reflects the grandeur, wonder, and glory of God. Model character in your daily living and teach Christian virtue through the life, death, burial, and resurrection of Jesus Christ.

Father God, may your Spirit empower me through the
blood of Christ to walk in a manner that is worthy of your
call, for you called me.

True peace comes
from seizing the
invitation to live a
God-centered life.

IDENTITY

Jesus said to them, "Truly, truly, I say to you, the Son can do nothing of his own accord, but only what he sees the Father doing. For whatever the Father does, that the Son does likewise."

JOHN 5:19 ESV

Jesus found his identity in the Father. Sons will grasp their value and worth by the display of love, grace, and affection that is afforded to them by their earthly fathers. Yet our earthly fathers often fail us and fall short of this lofty ideal.

As you look to Christ, the founder and perfecter of your faith, let the river of life flow from him into you with a constant current. This will form and establish a foundation for a Christ-centered identity that is firmly grounded in truth. Usher yourself to the foot of the cross so that you may find your creative purpose in the one who grants purpose.

Lord Jesus, I thank you that your sacrificial love granted me access to be called a child of God. Help me to find my value and worth in you.

STOREHOUSE OF WEALTH

I have stored up your word in my heart,
that I might not sin against you.
PSALM 119:11 ESV

In an age of information, may the fountain of your lips be filled with the Word of God. May the truth of his Word flow from your mouth into the hearts of those around you. How gracious would God be to allow your daily usage of words to be filled with his lifegiving truths. And how equally amazing would he be to have your friends and family be recipients of such treasures.

Be intentional about centralizing the Scriptures in your life and model a seriousness in handling the text. Saturate the minds of your loved ones. Be a storehouse of beauty that exudes truth to all you encounter.

Lord Jesus, incline my heart to your ways and etch in my mouth your words. Stir in me a great adoration for the Scriptures that overflows into the hearts and minds of the people in my life.

GRATEFUL HEARTS

*Children are a heritage from the LORD,
the fruit of the womb a reward.*

PSALM 127:3 ESV

Many men treat their cars with extra care and precision because they understand the value and worth of the vehicle. The Scriptures tell us that children are a blessing from the Lord. They embody the miracle of life that only God can provide while resembling his beauty, majesty, and grandeur.

Take a moment to reflect upon the children that God has brought into your life; whether they are sons, nephews, neighbors, or the ones that always seem to scamper underfoot throughout the church foyer. Realize that God has granted you the opportunity to show these children that their lives have value, dignity, and worth.

Father God, It is by your grace that I'm granted the privilege to be called a child of God. My value and worth are intrinsically rooted in who I am in you.

RESPECT

Hear, my son, your father's instruction,
and forsake not your mother's teaching.

PROVERBS 1:8 ESV

Respect for authority is a trait learned by observing a father who lives it well. The value of community and the profit of parents is understood by the tutelage and guidance of a fatherly figure. No earthly father is perfect, but when submitted to God they will instill a posture of respect that will permeate their entire family.

Take some time today to reflect upon the father that God gave to you. What instruction did he provide that you carry with you to this day?

Lord Jesus, remind me of the instruction that my father provided. Help me to overlook his shortcomings and view him as you want me to see him.

Choices made today
impact the pathways
for tomorrow.

SUPREMACY OF CHRIST

Since therefore the children share in flesh and blood, he himself likewise partook of the same things, that through death he might destroy the one who has the power of death that is, the devil.

HEBREWS 2:14 ESV

Children have an innate ability to sense the inaccuracy of ordinary life. As we age, it is essential that we bring to the forefront the colossal shortcomings that surface, in order to magnify the supremacy of the cross.

The charge for men is not to sweep these blunders under the rug but to recognize that the cross of Christ cleanses us from all discrepancies. Though the sinfulness of our hearts can be heinous and, at times, unbearable, the magnitude of the cross conveys the message that the love of Christ stretches as far as the east is from the west.

Lord Jesus, teach me to rest at the foot of your cross where salvation, restoration, and reconciliation are found.

LOVE THE CHURCH

*By this we know that we love the children of God, when we
love God and obey His commandments.*

1 JOHN 5:2 ESV

Model a great affinity toward the community
of saints. This is sustained not by the self-generated
will, but by a proper perspective of the biblical scope
inflamed by the Holy Spirit. Being infused into the
local assembly of saints will grant you the capacity to
see life in God's larger scale.

Service to the children of God will create a
disposition that will align you with God's redemptive
work in using the church to bring forth restoration
through Jesus Christ. We all long to be part of
something that is greater than ourselves. It is through
the church that the manifold wisdom of God might
now be made known to the rulers and authorities in the
heavenly places.

*Lord Jesus, grant me an affection for your people that I
may faithfully serve them for your name.*

TRANSPARENCY

If we confess our sins, he is faithful and just to forgive us our sins and to cleanse us from all unrighteousness.
1 JOHN 1:9 ESV

Real strength is not an innate or self-generated sustenance; rather, it is grounded in a deep dependency on God. Confession of sin acknowledges the inability of the self and gravitates toward the one true God who sustains, restores, and redeems.

As a man, it is imperative to demonstrate the humility of confession, first to the Lord and second to your friends and family, which will embody a transparency that evokes the fruit of the Spirit. Not only does it demonstrate the supremacy of Christ in your life, but it also models a clear picture of gospel living.

Lord Jesus, help me to not lean on my own righteousness. Teach me humility.

FOLLOW HIS FOOTSTEPS

Whoever says he abides in Him ought to walk in the same way in which He walked.

1 JOHN 2:6 ESV

As a young athlete, you may have watched one of the greatest basketball players in the world—Michael Jordan. After an intense and gripping game, you may have even found yourself at the local court, shooting fadeaways and attempting acrobatic lay-ups with your tongue hanging out.

We are not to become our own man per se; we are to mimic and imitate the God-man himself. He has come to show us what true humanity looks like, and by his Spirit we are to emulate him. As you walk through the day, ask the Spirit to align your heart with his ways for his glory.

Lord Jesus, grant me the favor to walk in your ways. Incline my heart and stir my affections to your truth.

RELATIONSHIPS

As iron sharpens iron,
so a friend sharpens a friend.
PROVERBS 27:17 NLT

This verse from Proverbs produces strong mental imagery. One can almost see the blacksmith's hammer poised momentarily above his head before it descends with a resounding clang on the glinting broadside of a dull sword. There is a seemingly violent and almost destructive nature to this process of iron sharpening iron. What an interesting picture chosen to represent friendship.

Do you have iron in your life? That person who either attacks or defends in any given situation. It is these seemingly more contentious relationships that sharpen our character. As we parry with them, our arguments are honed and convictions solidified. If nothing else, they give us opportunities to practice patience, forgiveness, and grace.

God, help me to love the people you have placed in my life for the purpose of sharpening.

HOLINESS

Strive for peace with everyone, and for the holiness without which no one will see the Lord.

<small>HEBREWS 12:14 ESV</small>

Autonomous identity is what society etches into the minds and hearts of its people. Uniqueness is pursued in order to stand out, be distinct, and find ourselves in a class of our own. Yet what the biblical data conveys is a wholeness that is contingent upon linking oneself to the Creator, which brings forth a sanctity that sets us apart.

Holiness is obtained through a divine union with him through the work and person of Jesus Christ. Our distinction from the world is our disposition to live counterculturally and to embody the new nature that is grounded in the Spirit.

Lord Jesus, thank you for your sacrificial love, which granted me salvation. Transform my heart so it is sensitive to your truth.

Wholeness is
contingent upon
linking yourself
to the Creator.

GROW IN MATURITY

Flee youthful passions and pursue righteousness, faith, love, and peace, along with those who call on the Lord from a pure heart.

2 TIMOTHY 2:22 ESV

Biblical manhood is not saturated with shallow definitions of bench press markings, sexual prowess, or financial achievement. A godly man is defined by his Christlike attitude that is expressed in consistent sacrificial servitude for the good of others and the joy of their hearts.

Maturing men seek to grow in pouring themselves out for the development of their loved ones while continuously being poured into through the mercies of the gospel. Righteousness, genuine faith, selfless love, and gentle peace are characteristics that describe the mark of a godly man.

Lord Jesus, help me to grow into the man you have called me to be. Align my heart with your purposes. Grant me steadfastness in your truth.

SUBMIT TO MENTORSHIP

*Follow the pattern of the sound words that you have heard
from me, in faith and love that are in Christ Jesus.*

2 TIMOTHY 1:13 ESV

You can only lead as far as you are being led!
The task of leadership is not for the faint of heart.
To properly take hold of the mandate to shine forth
the character of Christ, you must be undergirded by
the guidance of a biblically saturated individual who
engages the blind spots of life.

Find solid men to surround yourself with. Growth
occurs by being with people who will challenge you.
Scripture says, "Whoever walks with the wise becomes
wise, but the companion of fools will suffer harm"
(Proverbs 13:20).

*Lord Jesus, bring into my life a mentor who will point
me toward you. Help me to trust and open myself to his
critique. Bring forth growth and development that will
honor your name.*

TRAINING FOR A MARATHON

Rather train yourself for godliness.
1 Timothy 4:7 esv

"Rome wasn't built in a day."

"Olympic athletes don't shatter world records on their first day."

"Ball games are won in the off season."

"Preparation allows you to play fast."

All these sayings are marks, within athletic or warlike scenarios, which paint a picture of process. Though we are sold on the motto "quicker is better," the spiritual development of the heart takes time. Don't take shortcuts in your sanctity, and don't despise the process. Buckle yourself in for the long haul and embrace the fact that you are a work in progress.

Lord Jesus, grant me patience to endure my own personal development. Help me to keep my eyes on you, that I might not measure myself against anything else.

SEARCH THE INTENTIONS

*The aim of our charge is love that issues from a pure heart
and a good conscience and a sincere faith.*

1 TIMOTHY 1:5 ESV

Be sensitive to the motives of your heart and
keep watch on the intentions of your deeds. Saturate
yourselves with the person of Christ, that his love
might manifest itself in sacrificial deeds that will be a
fragrant offering and sacrifice to God.

Center your aim on the gospel, using the cross of
Christ as the model to measure all your expressions
of love. Look toward the cross to find his goodness.
The sweetness of his love can be the standard of your
actions.

*Lord Jesus, search the depths of my heart and reveal the
severity of my sin.*

THANKFULNESS

We ought always to give thanks to God for you, brothers beloved by the Lord, because God chose you as the first fruits to be saved, through sanctification by the Spirit and belief in the truth.

2 THESSALONIANS 2:13 ESV

Gratitude postures the heart to not terminate one's thoughts, ambitions, and goals, but to see the gifts that have been given, ultimately, by God. In turn, we'll live in a manner that brings him praise.

There is a tendency to be inwardly focused and, as a result, meditate upon all the things that we don't have. Thankfulness, on the contrary, centers its attention on the Blesser who has given to us beyond all comprehension. Eternal life. Bountiful meals. Amazing shelter. A beautiful family. Be thankful that in his providence you are blessed beyond comparison.

Lord Jesus, stir in me a heart of gratitude. Help me to be aware of your blessings in my life.

HOLINESS THROUGH GOD

God has not called us for impurity, but in holiness.
1 THESSALONIANS 4:7 ESV

In an age of relativism, saturate your mind with a robust biblical view of the triune God of the universe. Do not settle for small glimpses of him but be filled in awe with the mighty pictures that Scripture paints of our Creator.

Meditate on the distinction between the creation and the Creator. Marvel at the notion that he is everlasting, and we are merely a mist within the wind. Ground yourself with the idea that the confines of time are not able to restrain him.

Lord Jesus, grant me the desire to capture a clear understanding of you. May my thoughts of you be full of substance and richness.

A godly man is defined by his Christlike attitude, expressed in consistent sacrificial servitude.

MARINATE

Let the Word of Christ dwell in you richly, teaching and admonishing one another in all wisdom, singing psalms and hymns and spiritual songs, with thankfulness in your hearts to God.

COLOSSIANS 3:16 ESV

We serve and lead out of the wealth that is stored up in our hearts. The value of life that permeates from our lives is intrinsically linked to the life that is within us. This life is not inherently ours; it's the breath of God that is blown into us through his Word.

Saturate yourself with his breath and continue to root yourself in the life source of God through the living Word. Only then can you begin to serve in such a way as to have the eternal impact that God has designed for you.

Lord Jesus, grant me a hunger and thirst for your Word, so my heart would be a fountain that stores your truth. May the words that flow from my mouth be filled with life.

UNITING LOVE

Above all these put on love, which binds everything together in perfect harmony.

COLOSSIANS 3:14 ESV

As men, we tend to lean toward one of two extremes: over-discipline or under-discipline. Some of us have a natural tendency toward being overdisciplined because we strive for perfection. We seek to maintain order often at the expense of being harsh with ourselves and those around us. Others prefer an underdisciplined lifestyle because they fall prey to laziness or don't want to deal with the responsibilities of life.

The biblical perspective brings balance that is produced by a sacrificial love, grounded in the commandments. Embody a Christlikeness that expresses itself in grace and truth.

Lord Jesus, may your Spirit bring forth unity that expresses itself in love. May the impulse of my heart be to personify your compassion, mercy, and grace.

ANXIETY STEALS

Do not be anxious about anything, but in everything by prayer and supplication with thanksgiving let your request be made known to God.

PHILIPPIANS 4:6 ESV

Today, the pressures of getting there (wherever there is) is the undergirding drive and influence that stimulates a posture of anxiety that steals the beauty of the now. What will best serve your own heart is the ability to strive toward God's purpose while simultaneously embracing your current season of life. Don't look ahead at the price of neglecting what the Lord has blessed you with now.

Whether you are in a season of sorrow or joy, plenty or want, chaos or peace, make the best use of the time and live each day with a zeal for the Lord.

Lord Jesus, forgive me for not trusting you. Posture my heart in a fashion of hope that grounds itself in you.

CHRIST-CENTERED AIM

*I press on toward the goal for the prize of the upward call
of God in Christ Jesus.*
PHILIPPIANS 3:14 ESV

It's imperative to see and understand the principles that drive the things we seek to do and accomplish in life. It's not enough to merely go through the motions; we need to continuously evaluate the motives and intentions of our heart in order to clearly see the motivating factors that fuel our life.

Without such evaluation, we will begin to place a weight upon our family, friends, or coworkers that they are not meant to carry. We must fight valiantly to keep at center the person and work of Jesus Christ. Without such admonition, we are bound to crush the very people we love.

Lord Jesus, search the depths of my heart and incline my mind to your ways. May I meditate upon your precepts and find joy in your commands.

DISRUPTIVE PERVERSION

Sexual immorality and all impurity or covetousness must not even be named among you, as is proper among saints.

EPHESIANS 5:3 ESV

The institution of marriage is meant to display the beauty and mystery of God's redeeming work in reconciling the church to himself. The nucleus of the family is a shadow of God's eternal inheritance fulfilled in the person of Christ. All these images are to be compounded in the kingdom of God.

Sexual immorality is the attempt of the evil one to destroy, thwart, and diminish God's redemptive picture. The health and vitality of your family, present or future, points far beyond your own personal achievements, navigating and finding its fulfillment in the majesty of the triune God. Turn your thoughts to the Lord and flee from impurity.

Lord Jesus, help me to see the world through your eyes, that the actions of my heart would point to your creative purpose and design.

LOVE IS A PERSON

God is love.
1 JOHN 4:8 ESV

Love is not merely an affection, a concept, or a devotion; rather, it finds its grounding in the person of Jesus Christ. Our society communicates the essence of love as an emotive principle that is gauged by the individual, but God's Word forges a different reality.

Love is unified with truth in the person of Jesus. Christ entered the tapestry of creation full of grace and truth. He is the standard by which we are to grasp and understand the power of love. Immerse yourself in the person of Christ and find yourself exemplifying the love that governs the universe.

Lord Jesus, forgive me for chasing concepts and principles. Holy Spirit, help me to chase after Christ, that I would grow in my love and affection toward him.

Love finds its
grounding in
the person of
Jesus Christ.

RIGHTEOUSNESS OF CHRIST

*Filled with the fruit of righteousness that comes through
Jesus Christ, to the glory and praise of God.*
PHILIPPIANS 1:11 ESV

A caricature of the Christian faith is the moralistic
approach to the law. Though God's commandments
are important to the faith, they are not the entry point
to which union with Christ is obtained. The grounds
on which the saints will stand before an infinitely
holy God are cemented not in righteousness that is
harbored innately, but through righteousness found in
Christ.

When we come to grips with the fact that our
right standing with God is dependent upon Christ's
fulfillment of the law, we will begin to walk in humility,
not only toward the Creator, but also toward those we
encounter daily. Your righteousness is not your own.

*Lord Jesus, help me to yearn for your righteousness, that
the outflow of my heart would be the righteousness that
brings you glory.*

MANNER OF LIFE

Let your manner of life be worthy of the gospel of Christ.
PHILIPPIANS 1:27 ESV

One's belief system governs the external expression of life. Verbal commitments are shallow without a proper response in conduct, commitment, and propriety. In actuality, the common thread that is produced in one's exterior engagement communicates a definitive posture of the heart.

In order to properly establish a manner of life worthy of the gospel of Christ, one must abide in his Word.

Lord Jesus, teach me to hunger for your Word, that the meditations of my heart would be saturated with your truth.

SUFFERING

It has been granted to you that for the sake of Christ you should not only believe in him but also suffer for his sake.

PHILIPPIANS 1:29 ESV

The tendency of this age is to question God's goodness in the midst of suffering. Yet suffering is the means by which God conforms us into the image of the Son. When bad things happen in our lives, may we not ask, "Why me?" but rather, "What are you teaching me?"

If in Christ there is no condemnation, then the suffering we face is not necessarily God's judgment. We can be assured that for those who love God, all things work together for good.

Lord Jesus, forgive me for pursuing my comfort over your glory. Teach me to walk in obedience even if it means I must endure suffering.

HEART POSTURE

Do all things without grumbling or disputing.
PHILIPPIANS 2:14 ESV

As a believer of Jesus Christ, posture your heart in a manner that seeks to bring praise and honor to the Lord. As his child, put on his character and walk in his meekness. It should be your aim that in whatever you do, you work hard as if for the Lord and not for men.

The intention of your heart is as important as the conduct of your behavior. Submit them both to him.

Lord Jesus, incline my heart to your ways, that I may walk in contentment and serve in joy. May the posture of my heart be to see you glorified.

MORE OF HIM

That I may know him and the power of his resurrection, and may share his sufferings, becoming like him in his death.

PHILIPPIANS 3:10 ESV

Mimicking Jesus may not necessarily produce success from a worldly standpoint. Reorienting our expectations and redefining advancement is necessary in understanding true success which is more about conformity to the image of Christ and less about worldly recognition.

When we view the world through the gospel lens, we find that trends do not dictate a faithful service to God, but rather one's commitment to being his disciple.

Lord Jesus, teach me that you are my end goal. Sharpen my eyes to see that you are not a means to another end, but rather you are the end to my means.

COSTLY LOVE

God shows his love for us in that while we were still sinners,
Christ died for us.
ROMANS 5:8 ESV

Love, service, and discipleship without cost do not resemble the formation of gospel-saturated love. As the world continues to fight for convenience, embrace the sacrificial love that is personified through Jesus Christ.

Giving of yourself is posturing your heart in accordance with God in order to convey the message of the gospel through deeds in service to others. In this way, you will mimic the Creator who so loved the world that he gave his only Son, that whoever believes in him should not perish but have eternal life.

Lord Jesus, forgive me when I serve you out of convenience. Remind me of how your call to discipleship is a call to death. Holy Spirit, help me see that living for you is more valuable than my comfort.